ALL

All

ROBERT POWELL

Valley Press

First published in 2015 by Valley Press
Woodend, The Crescent, Scarborough, YO11 2PW
www.valleypressuk.com

First edition, first printing (January 2015)

ISBN 978-1-908853-44-8
Cat. no. VP0063

A CIP record for this book is available from the British Library.

Printed and bound in the EU by Pulsio, Paris.

www.valleypressuk.com/authors/robertpowell

Contents

3. ALL

Acknowledgements

Some of these poems have previously appeared in *The Horse's Mouth*, *Orbis*, *Pennine Platform* and *The Rialto*. 'Owls in Dusk' won the Elmet Poetry Prize at the Ted Hughes Festival 2012, judged by Kathleen Jamie. My thanks to all the poets who helped me hone many of these poems in workshops coordinated in Wakefield and York by John I. Clarke, Margaret Speak, Carole Bromley, and Nicholas Bielby, and Josie Walsh; and also to Jamie McGarry of Valley Press for his support and close attention.

for Dianne, Owen & Hugh

& in memory of David Arthur Callard,
Michael Taylor, and Glyn Hughes

1. *The Strange Places*

The Poet Knocked

for Alan Jackson

The poet knocked on my door
as I sat dreaming at my desk
in that summer of hesitation
while the heron landed the dusk.

The desk was made from a door
which was open and shut forever
and in case of heartbreak or fire
would fly to the river, where

another place would be waiting,
a house that was safe for the heart,
a heart-house safe, save
for the risk of drowning

in dreams that could turn
from cliché to danger,
like certain words
and the lives lived near them.

> *I have things to say*
> > *that I know you've forgotten,*
> *I have her address*
> > *and the map to her heart,*
> *I know the way*
> > *to the path to your joy,*
> *and all you could be*
> > *if only you started;*

the road through the forest,
the place of the key,
the way you can make
the locked lands free

He knocked again
and he knocked again.
As though stood behind him,
out there in the garden,

I could see him hammer:
that small, tense shape
of sad, fierce hunger
at the locked red door.

I didn't answer,
sat still and waited.
The heron and the summer flew
and only now do I know what I knew.

Snapshot

Picture this: in a shock of light
you're there, motionless, with a strange
white dog staring up at you in surprise
as if it's just seen a ghost,
or a huge bone, or a bomb
beginning to flower behind you,
in the second before everything
is thrown into the future.

But you know there's no ghost, bomb, or bone
in that unearthly glare at your back –
just the restless foetus of the sun,
its dreaming cast across the frost-seized field
to the horizon before you.
And, stretched over this pale sheet
three shadows, perfectly paralyzed – of you, the dog,
and a many-branched tree.

It's as if what you once took for granted
has come back and slapped you in the face;
or like an image from childhood
that returns after some thing
seemingly small in the day
drops at your feet – a dark, thrown
present that gives you one more chance
to notice you're here and nowhere else.

And you know that in another breath
it will all pass, something will shatter it –

the dog will tear off with its fur full of burrs
of bounding hope, a sudden bird start from the grass,
or a cloud pass, like free will. Or a mobile phone will sound
and it will be a voice on a train asking someone
to put the kettle on, or a multinational company
making you another offer.

Ignore them. Let the sun warm your back,
feel it slip through your hair like a lover's fingers
and melt the pressed frost in your footprints
as one by one you abandon them.
Climb the shadow of that tree
as it shrinks over the clearing ahead.
Go on, allow. If you're lucky,
that strange dog will follow.

No One and Nothing

No one and nothing is ordinary.
Young Stalin, beautifully, sings in the choir.
Because she loves them, Christine
stores her dead cats in the freezer.
A worker stands in construction mud
whistling badly in his own flawless way.
And my grandfather, after years selling life
insurance, painted intricate clichés on canvas;
but also a winter wood you can walk in.

And so with things:
a single pebble gains sudden fame
buried deep in the forehead
of a big celebrity, but others
have talent too;
strong silent types, secret rock stars
holding geologies in place; the edges
and molten places; mountains, shores,
reason.

So now – when soft
and seemingly generic wind sifts
through this summer doorway
on a slow grey afternoon you,
with apparent justice, could call everyday –
you look up, quick,
and a perfectly black blackbird arcs past
in a billion generations of wings
just once, one time.

The Wakening

You woke in the crowded restaurant
with some people you knew, you thought – and not
for the first time recently he was involved, although not
present. You were sure it had all been so carefully planned:
the suitcase left at the small house on the far side of the foreign city,
you'd pick it up in plenty of time, and they were serving intricate tiny cakes with some
familiar names written on them by children in seeds or smoke or whatever – and realizing you
were late and wouldn't make it to the plane already sitting on the runway in the rain
where your lover waited, and since public transport, though preferable
for the planet, was now out of the question, you left too quickly,
while attempting to retain a semblance of dignity, to look
for a taxi on a broad avenue full of strange yet beautiful
traffic and trees at dusk, or perhaps early morning,
something like life.

Light Passing Across an Ancient City

after a series of paintings by Jake Attree

Imagine an ancient city,
and wherever you walk or sleep
it is there, unbroken, loud and traffic-filled,
even in the forests, ancient and new as the seed
of the Tree of Wisdom; the great family tree that buds
    forever,
its fruit dropping constantly into the street
outside your door.

Of course this city has a river
for the sad refugees of water fleeing the high places,
sierras, mountains and moors,
longing for their young mother with her tears of salt;
Ouse and Thames, Seine, Nile, Yangtze and Lethe,
with bridges for the boys of summer to leap from, laughing,
into the current of time.

And here looms
the great minster, mosque-like,
its pale towers and hollows shot through
with the multi-coloured pigments of hope,
and all around it tesserae, roofs of slate and stone
and clay and gingerbread, stretching to where
the surprised castle sleeps beneath its baled hill.

Here the young look for themselves restlessly in the old
    places;
the hunters trudge home; peasants doze in the corn,
    awaiting

the herd's return from yesterday; lonely shoppers graze
    in the shadows
of the temple walls, mud and bodies and beasts and
    water all shifting before them
and before us, through the darkening spaces, through
    the screen
of trees at the edge of the wood, in harvests of light,
    here, not here,
in the ancient city.

Where is this city?
What is its name?
Atlantis, where they swim slowly to the office,
or Helike, which sank at night in the winter of 373 BC,
Eboracum, Pompeii, El Dorado, Ville d'Ys,
Camelot, Piramesse,
in the street outside your door.

And at dawn in your sleep you turn over,
the paintings on the walls shut their eyes again,
the fading brushes of headlights stroke the ceiling,
and leaves flicker on the charcoal-bright river
like hands waving greeting and goodbye,
fallen with the light, light
passing across the ancient city.

The Duties of Stones

Saint-Guilhem-le-Désert

Some to fly high
in the company of birds,
feathers in their caps,
some in foundations, others on show,
some to be under and some on top,
though most
somewhere in the middle.

Placed here by ghosts, each
with its fingerprints handed a role,
mossy or dry, this one tavern
this one shop, street, tower, wall,
clenching the river, saying no
to the sheep, gripping the roof-trees
and their stone-coloured leaves;

some to whisper there is nothing,
others that there is something,
shaping the rain, preventing
the hills from tumbling
on the tourists' heads,
some bearing up, others down,
and all held fast in the weight

of what is, in the gravity
of their situation, layer
on layer, sequential as music,

dependent on each other
like acrobats, allowing
that bridge to leap in three long arcs
a thousand years over the gorge.

Yet there's always one,
at least one – maybe right here
where the wood lintel sags
above our window, love,
preparing to slip
back to the stony earth
where birdshadows sail.

This Autumn Light

for Josie Walsh

This autumn light that catches in the throat
lives at the eyes' edges, under the brows
of the trees, and in the late western sky slices
into the body of the city.

One leaf falls and then another
onto the rushing cars, the graves, the child's shoe,
as she stands gazing into the churchyard and the
     glimmering dusk
of her own possibilities. She lifts her bicycle over the stone,

feels safe here, will stay minutes, possibly hours. The sun
     sets
but light continues to grow everywhere – in her breast,
in the bricks and bones; the strangely bright architecture
of everything becoming night,

the rushing windscreens full of now, the gutters of before,
dogs barking at the shadows of old worlds
from their deep heritage of warning at the boundaries
of small places, buried gateposts, the outskirts

of villages, the many walls between people,
what they own and she owns and what you own, or can call
     yours,

and now she feels again the sad tug at her heart,
her grandmother's voice calling her home.

At a Yorkshire Wedding in London

for Matthew & Karen

1.

You stride into the river: manly, nine, fearless
at its deep, calm-seeming face
under the rooted cliff.
Hair white, back and legs pale as the bellies of fish,
the passing ancient river drinks you in,
its darkness licks your skin;
in the world with no age the other waits –
then you burst back up to us, and grin.

*

And as for you: ten, in your sulking skirt outlandish,
you brandish Duran Duran near the gate
to the cricket club. Your high forehead under ginger gorse
ripples with curiosity as your life, in a glint,
stretches whole before you, like a horse
racing along the sky, or like water
in a long reservoir in the moor wind; and the other
just a fleck on it, a blur, an unborn seed in a wave.

*

A small river, this one, where edge-water slips
like see-through muscle over the stones,
peat-dyed, ale-brown, down from the vast highways
of moors. Just above, two streams join at the crotch
of two valleys. You could call it a kind of sex –
distances couple, double DNAs of heather, light,
and rain writhe on each other like lovers' limbs
wrestling to be one.

*

This place you come from is hard, hand-made.
Its young stagger in the streets on rivers buried
under sardonic tarmac slapped over setts
laid one by one for iron wheels, hooves, clogs, the bare
feet of children, and the bared minting of brass
from muck; while high above them, stacked libraries of stone
lie in lines on sleeping horizons,
holding the hills in their place, unread.

2.

Here, all the fires
are out.

North, as ever,
hides its wounds
and tears, drinks
down the loss
of its brightest sparks
drained south.

*

We start apart, dropped
into the stream of others.
What happens next
is only guessed or hoped.

Waters rush,
there are surfaces,
and things under surfaces –
beneath the map, the other map:

the golden stone unwrapped
that blackens in the air,
the golden stone that rests below
and dreams on the dark stair.

*

So go, loves, flow.
Love doubled, go.

Methodist

Eight stone walls and a roof of stone
to hold the hills and sky at bay, the rain away,
and the cloughs in their places; so many facets to face
the gusts or God, no matter their fierce directions.

Inside, the silence of a felled forest: box pews
like lidless coffins in a sculpted boat of wood
to bear the souls fished from hand-looms, brand-new
mills, and the paralysed sea of moors, to Paradise.

Here, the perched slab of the black bible
laid on the pulpit to preach to a stopped clock
in the smell of the imprisoned mystery
of damp hope, big as a small tombstone;

and there, the ghosts
packed like coping stones in steep balconies
under the clouds, awaiting again the sermon
about the fish, or the one about wrath...

> *The end of all flesh is come before me*
> *And behold I, even I, do bring a flood of waters*
> *upon the earth*

And you too receive a text,
soundless from heaven:

> *Where r u?*
> *Call me now r l8r*
> *i still luv u*

The orders have changed, but some faiths
and fears remain. The door's unlocked
all day, but just inside,
the hand-scrawled note:

> *Keep Door Closed*
> *To Keep Cats Out*
>
> *(Bless You)*

Fugitive

for Charles Simic

At the Eastman Kodak Museum
in Rochester, New York, in 1985
they believed they possessed
a rare photograph
contained in a silver
case the size
of a small Victorian
woman's palm,
which they were afraid
to open.

In the lengthening shadows
of a late summer
afternoon with trees waving
silently in the window
the Director sat
in his office, the case
on the polished desk
before him:

It's the light, he said.
If we look inside
we're very worried
that the image we've never seen
might disappear.

Her Name, Remember

St. Agnes, Cornwall, 2012

was Lesley, across the curving bar
though what you notice first are her eyes,
cyan-blue and sort of *faraway, man*, which was *cool*,
and then her breasts, nestled in her blouse like sleeping
seabirds while she pulls you a pint; her rounded hips,
her back to you and her tilting backbone at the till,
her harbour lips and smile with its slightly-chipped tooth
as she gives you the change, fingers brushing your hand,
and moves on.

And later she, Lindsey, comes over for a chat in the lee
of the huge stone fireplace under the inn beams.
Her earrings gleam in the lick of the flames.
Outside, it's January in Cornwall, the sea cracks
on the nearby rocks, but here with her it's a tropic of
Capricorn, she says, her *star-sign*, and that time,
and her signals, all pulling you to a place
you'd rather be, you think, than where you are.
O Lesley…

Or was it Linda? Her image haunted you for days,
a wick of warmth aglow in bleak midwinter on that coast
of wind and tedious wild air, and you felt like a sailor
and she a lightship, until at last you could stand it
no longer, sailed the bitter three miles of fields
to the place where she lived, Linda, Lesley;
a caravan at Tretharmen with her macho mechanic boyfriend
on whom, it's obvious, she was completely and utterly
wasted.

Linda I love you! you said – or was it Lesley? –
and meant it; like a seed in a storm, would have thrown
away everything (which in those days wasn't much)
gone with her to Canada, that cabin by the lake,
or Paris, Guadalajara, Wyoming, Avalon
or Barnstaple, and lived in houses you haven't entered, with
    windows
looking out over unknown streets and gardens, in sites
    unseen,
made friends with strangers, had those other
children –

but Lindsey said no. Years later
you're at that seaside inn again, curved bar, stone fireplace,
twisted beams salvaged, they say, from the wrecks of
    Spanish ships,
seabirds in stuffed glass cases, replica weapons on the walls,
    the usual –
and standing in the night, tide scrolling down the beach
in darkness far below, from behind your two sons,
in the lit doorway, Lesley Lindsey Linda
smiling, older but with blue eyes, faraway,
doesn't appear.

Memorial

Scarborough, 2008

Such a long, fine walk along the coast,
on familiar paths we had never seen,
while the cliffs leaked light back
into the formidable sky.

> *Will you walk with me again?*

On the cliffs it was winter, but the sea,
like memory, has no seasons,
which is why the dead
live so well in it.

> *Will you walk with me again?*

I can't tell you where they're gone,
each with his pardons and her reasons:
the restless, constant surface
slides before us, and away.

> *Walk with me again.*

The Missing Child

Even now they are looking for me
in the still present, still opening petals
of that summer afternoon,
storm at its edges, bruised
clouds in the metal sky
over the far shore, glint
of finned cars on the beach,
and from their open doors a voice
begging Diana to *O please stay*
while beneath the pines the boys
are all leaving, plunging
from the rocks
for kicks and two-cent bottles,
over and over, headlong.

I had no choice:
the force and beauty
of your words drew me
into the deeper water where weather stirred
from another world.
I couldn't help it, couldn't remain above
in the warmth and the measurement.
You pulled and I was transformed,
became other, half-hidden for good
in the cold spectacular reeds
beneath the surface of the lake
of my own skin.

So they searched and they called,
the old phones rang in rooms all over the city
and police cars, inevitably black and white,
cruised the horizons until night.

And they are still looking for me,
but I was no longer there.

I was here,
writing this.

2. *The Rivers Unfenced*

Fishing at an Unfenced River

i.m. Neil Armstrong

Here are the long voyaging
muscles of water, flexed
with the force of moon,
winding in slow afternoon
through drowned roots.

With time in their hands – near
enough to touch, yet poles apart –
these two squat in silence
on the bank, patiently awaiting the river's
ancient speech of silvery verbs.

But river texts now
in strange new tongues all
around them, behind their backs,
over their heads, thrusting through
shopped streets, past churches
with black walls flecked
by rose-brown rocks, smooth
as the insides of seashells,
transformed into nightclubs,
and past the great cathedral
spell-bound in its dumb dictionary
of stone.

So which language
can we use now to speak
of what is given and remains,

who we are together,
the sky's cold limits of blue,
and what the world may hold
beyond the world?

Rivers link earth and sky
here, not here,
root, cloud, and flood
on in their deep grooves,
continually just in time –
and at their edges,
empty footprints full of space
that silt and silence shuttle through.

The Luck of Rain

and the luck of leaves in the wind
The luck of the litter
The luck of meeting you – you, not her
The luck of being born there, not here
The luck of being born
The luck of that song
That song from the radio from the open window
and the luck of that window being open
The luck of the house still being there, and of you walking
    past it
just later, not then
so that the children could come
The children, and not just any children
but they, those two,
and not the third
The luck of the third
The luck of fear
The luck of insurance ads
of new inventions and mortgages
The luck of that train and its fixed journey
The luck of the jet exploding in mid-air
The luck of seeds
of looks that are seeds
of looks that become endless
The luck of being prepared
and the luck of being unprepared
The luck of plans
The luck of all
of all this.

The pure luck.

Witness

I remember he paused,
legs apart and slightly
tip-toed, arms
wide, as though
he wished to leap
from the world
or maybe just
embrace the car

and so stop it.
He did the first
then came back down
onto the road,
in the rain,
but sadly for him
and worse for me
he could not enter the world again.

Shipwreck

Perhaps the smartest
jumped ship early,
drowned elsewhere.

We who remained
were tongue-tied,
could only stay
the course, care
for our hold of earth,
belay despair
(though we foresaw
the pale children stretched
in grey morning on the beach at Godrevy).

In time we found
our voices, learned prayer,
collected, coupled, prepared
at some point to greet
the hospital rocks.

Storm continued.
We gazed into the astonishing
depths we have been given,
sailed on, knew
it could have been worse:
we might have stayed young forever.

Youth

O'er aery cliffs and glittering sands,
How lightly then it flashed along —
Coleridge

Well-wrapped
in the wind, this woman
pointed helpfully down
the tilted cliff:
Kittiwake, Gannet, Guillemot, she called out
against their noise.

And out far
on the grey flat skin
of sea, strands of light
glittered golden, like banks
of solid sand beneath
the sky.

Yet to you they were dark.
I'd swim to them and think
I was saved,
but they'd be nothing –
and under my feet
the black vacuum of water.

No, I said,
right next to you
but as if from another place,
Think sun-fields, sun-drifts,
schools of mermaids with torches,
playing hide and seek.

You said:
They aren't playing.
They're drawing me down.
I'm drowning; and that light
is pouring up from their hair
at me.

Insomnia in the Garden Cabin

Six in the autumn dawn: I couldn't sleep. Next door
the Pole is already gone in his big car from the house
where two sisters lived for years, adrift, then left,
over the hills to shape metal for money. Falling
pears pummel the cabin roof like fists
and the house on the other side is empty too
waiting for its next occupant, winter. In ours
you lie curled around a vacancy both of us know
but won't name. Six thirty. Many who were here once
are gone. Measure the tenancies: strip the floors to fields
to woods and then savannah on the rich young earth,
long undersea. Our knowledge is big, not far or deep.
The rest is about the balance we can keep
when what happens happens after, and before, our sleep.

Andrew Talks of His Father in Paris

for A.J.

Andrew talks of his father
here in the afternoon
in the kitchen with its yellow ceiling
while August heat grips the city

in clenched air. At the window,
in the view that falls five floors
to a sunless court, I lean and listen.
A tyrant of the English public school sort

who in punishment as a child
would make him kneel on the floor under the sink
while he shaved, and once heaved him
and his brother to the top of a bedroom

wardrobe, then lay down and fell asleep.
Later he would kiss them and buy them toys.
Now we walk up the *Rue des Pyrenees*
and you're trying to break free of the story

even as you tell it; but this one has no end.
The monster vanishes into a dark room
in the earth, reappearing in photographs
where he claims the right to look ordinary forever

and trails a black film without length,
an endless reel that coils
through the years in every room, at each crossroad,
as you seek the approving nod, or even glance,

of a ghost. What right do they have to a quick
heart attack, hauling them from justice?
Dead such as these exhale on in a labyrinth that opens
here at our feet in the *parc des Buttes Chaumont*

or any sudden garden or street, at a meeting,
on your wife's skin, in the eyes of your children.
You crave and reject his respect, his touch.
You love your hate, hate your love.

Andrew, you winced and twisted
as we walked through the heat in Paris.
I'm sorry I forgot all this when I went against you.
I miss you. I've picked up the dark film.

Mid-Winter

I'm taking them,
these clear days
when soul steps out
over the frozen garden
grass and leaves
footprints written in frost,
which the blackbird sweeps

over, rising in thin blue air
to the roof of the cabin,
under which I'll sit with myself
aged 23 or 24, like old friends
who've met again after years
wandering far and away
from each other.

We talk and laugh and
trade stories for ages
until there's the soft rap
of a hand on the door,
and it's my son with a cup of tea
smoking in the winter sun,
or his lovely mother
with her evergreen-deep eyes,

or you, my young companion,
come curious from your grave,
old now, and the blackbird
flashes away, stuttering
its shrill histrionic warning,
and frost and prints retreat
into earth and air.

Visitors

Cornwall, 1973

And here we are, grouped in the chill
March air, in the photo taken by the guest
who never arrived. The cottage hunches behind us:

I think it's the beginning of the final week, and if so,
Kathy is about to leave. Maybe that's the occasion.
Her bag is packed – it waits just inside the white door

forever, while she stands next to you, practising her lostness,
the labyrinth of her hair dark by your shoulder.
Is that a faint smile? It's hard to say: smoke

from your cigarette, just exhaled, blurs
her small face, and the rest drifts an endless halo
over Justin's head as he hovers here, finer than paper

between my hands. Only the saxophone, which he cradles
    like a baby,
kept him for a while on earth, and sure enough his gaze is
    distant,
hooked by something moving fast away on the horizon.

As for Arthur, he holds the pipe he sports for *gravitas*
but as he bites the stem it forces a grin with a life of its own,
    impish,
as though amused at him, and all of us, everything.

And you: your hair falls straight, shirt open, a pale V of chest.
You're in that cool blue *oeuvrier* jacket I found in Brittany;
you've taken possession, worn it all winter.

In this world, of course, it's always going to be grey now
like Kathy's eyes, the sky, my red check shirt, and the sea-
    green
flares your daughters one day will die for.

My hand rests on your shoulder.
Daffodils lean at our feet,
tough as knives.

And holding the camera, as always, the invisible recorder,
in this case seeing nothing, being not there,
as we stood together briefly in the spring, frameless in the air.

Winter Let, Cornwall

i.m. Michael Taylor

1.

And two girls are with us in the cottage tonight;
Debbie and Norma, plucked hitching hopelessly
from the Truro road at dusk.

With their long hair they're lovely,
their clothes like rags from rainbows, and black
scored in Redruth, Falmouth, Saint Ives;
they're hungry, they can't remember,
Debbie has astonishingly green eyes and Norma
a sore right foot.

Now it's after midnight and you
have Norma in your bed, while Debbie sleeps
a few feet from me – I can feel her breath just here
through the ancient door, the heat from her skin,
the great Cornish wind wrapping and unwrapping
over the roof, fields, her closed face.

And three miles away in the dark, the sea's white teeth,
bare where it licks and thrusts in the night
at its old partner; while further out still a pale
and ludicrous ship, a woman on its plunging prow,
painted breasts open to the waves, and green eyes,
strikes rock and sinks.

2.

In that place we occupied so briefly, there were snails
which on the walls by day as still as fossils, by night
surveyed the surfaces of the universe, silver shoes
treading through the pinned, windless grasses
so meticulously mounted on brown paper I'd found in that
    empty mill,
in a box of dust, labelled with fine black strokes of ink

1917

                            1923

                1906

and this night, for no reason,
the moon allows that we're all still there –
the wind, the grass, the girls,
and that dream of the careless sea,
which for me remains three miles from a winter let,
but for you, old friend, is become home.

Just the Once

Kathy, I imagine just once
I catch you dancing
in the long wet garden
grass, to the dark, sharp music
of crows.

In those moments you become
all the dancers I have ever seen,
the dancer in me, the ones who danced
long before, and will dance
after the broken waters.

And although it is never now,
I know it was one late afternoon
just before Christmas,
dusk falling,
no lights in the cottage;

you were barefoot,
alien, like fire
uprooted, eyes shut,
hunting for your lost home,
by touch, along winter horizons.

Night in Tel Aviv

This is the hour of miracles
when the sun has left the land
and a lone Arab plucks the day's remains
from the beach, and chains the plastic orange
chairs, as if they might escape by night
to Egypt, or America.

Beyond the blinded neon vista
of the great bland hotels,
Sheraton, Metropolitan, Park Plaza,
far out in the dark mid-earth sea,
waves loosen, drift, pulse into the nape
of the bay, white, white necklaces on white.

It's the hour of miracles:
in anger a fisherman hurls a flounder
from Jaffa to Jerusalem; its fins glint
in the moonlight, the flight-paths, the options,
and in return, money and bread are thrown back –
and silence, a smothering net.

So the old deal still holds:
this hour and land and sea,
this bread, fish, money,
silence,
and this plenty;
this starving plenty.

How Bears Could Help Man Get to Mars

The Independent, 18th February 2011

It could happen like this –
your machines fail, we proliferate
unexpectedly quickly, come down
from the hills, scare
the shit out of you –
and you all leave.
No, the Moon isn't far enough,
it has to be at least Mars.

Or, it could happen like this –
we're all dead, which means
the insects, birds and fish are gone too,
the forests emptied and gone,
and the uprooted wind
is harvesting just dust
in your fallen cities.
You have no choices left:
the remaining rockets fly
with your Chosen Few.

Or, it could be like this –
in your sleep you are reunited
with your favourite Teddy and learn again
how to cry for your mother.
Or you're at the Teddy Bears' Picnic
in your bearskin hat, eating ants.
Then you go along the ridge
and enter the dark woods
that were once your home,

talking again to the trees,
and more than this, listening
to their answers.

In the house at the very heart,
where the windows all look out
onto the rest of your life,
the chairs open their arms,
the bowls are full and steaming,
the beds rest assured,
and you understand at last
that they have all been put here for you,
for us and for you, by us:
only by us.

The Dictator's Pleasure Yacht

after an art installation by Fernando Sanchez Castillo

At the former slaughterhouse of the great city,
in a vast cold storage room scorched by fire,
with walls and metal rafters blackened like barbecued ribs,
there float the remains of the former yacht
of the former dictator.

Once its armoured metal, masts and flags sailed gaily on
    summer seas
while the Leader, watched by his doting family,
sat in his special chair on deck, like any other good father
on holiday, proud, relaxed, fishing – and smiling, too,
for the blinded cameras.

He'd struggle to do the same now, for the simple (but always
    willing)
fish would need to rise to sacrifice themselves on his bright
    and friendly hooks
from beneath a concrete floor laid like a carapace over
    everything
and scored with gutters to drain away the blood of the
    creatures who hung here,
dreaming of meadows, horizons, and other political
    alternatives.

As for his pleasure yacht: abandoned for years and then as a
    floating casino
losing all bets, it was bought by this artist, scrapped and
    compressed
into four large metal cubes, chest-high – one, you could say,

for each of the corners of the country,
and placed here for all to see.

The curator reports that visitor opinion is divided.
Some see that their beloved Leader, who guided the nation
with such craft, has now acquired the status of Art;
others, also recalling, see only a pile of metal junk,
heavy with irony.

The concrete floor does not complain: after all,
both art and junk are better than blood, fire, hung bodies.
At night, when the old place is closed and everyone is in bed,
it sleeps, a sea without waves, still in the darkness,
awaiting the dawn.

Lost

We hear that the Tuareg of Africa
have lost the night sky.
They used to know
where it was, and what,
but they have lost it.

Now
when they look up
they see a vast black sheet
littered with bright holes.
They see a scattered crowd
of crazy blinking.

And they have also lost
the night sky's far language
its cold but helpful clues
its way of saying:
> *that way to Mecca,*
> *this way, home.*

They ask
their aging parents, who,
while the star-lit bushes
sway and whisper,
scratch their heads and mumble:
> *the old people*
> *used to talk about this…*

The Tuareg of Africa
have lost the night sky.
Still, at least they know
something is missing.

3. *All*

On Reading – 1

The page in the book,
held in the hand, with the fluttering blue
of the sky behind it glimpsed through birch trees:

   silver trees,
   whose turning leaves in the pale breeze
   sound like rain,

   rainfall fretting, felt or thought
   in a morning or memory that drifts like mist
   from the leaves onto a verandah,

   a green verandah,
   raised like a proscenium stage with curtains of blood-red
   ivy, but with no script, and actors who are not playing,

   strange actors,
   who are possibly your own parents posed, guilty with
      time, in a photograph
   where a newspaper, stirred by the breeze, sounds like
      rain,

   rain that is falling
   around this autumn place, in a story told by a character
      in a story
   from another country, in another season and century,

   a century composed
   of countless moments which flickered against a blue sky
   like faces in an old film, then vanished,

vanished, only to reappear
in a new time and place, a place where
there is just sufficient silence
to hear the voice of the light rain
from the birch trees,
on the page,
in the book;

this book, held
in this hand.

Owls in Dusk

Two darknesses more dense
than the scattered silhouettes
of leaves, in a sky not yet quite full night
but slow, deepening, ultramarine.
Your soft screams ripple out, old
into the pulsing tide
of car-hum, street voices, television
murmur from the semis' shallow windows.
A jet gleams in the distances behind you
and moon floods all, careless.

Holding a half-full cup I pause
to watch you in the chilled air
just beyond the lit door
of the house, neck-deep
in a threadbare dressing gown
and October.

Sixty-two years
and my two sons gone.
So who is this boy, thrilled
to see you tear quickly and go –
his eyes twin darknesses – and the
black up-flowing branches of night quiver?

Open

I love these mornings in the house where everything is
open. Night bees fly from the mouth, leaving, forgetting.
All the inner doors swing out, as if every sleeper has just
dressed and left. You open a radio and hear the great daily
news of water and gibberish and horizons. In a cupboard
birds awake, rattling the plates. Leaves pour in through the
letterbox.

They are rarer now, these mornings, but never came often.
In those days they were like walking out into a huge web
of light hung dazzled between the branches of clouds. Like
first love, you stepped into it half by accident and it was
destroyed. Sometimes they called up the smell of rain on
pavement under the pine trees, unseen and exciting like
the earlobes of girls, and you ran out of the school late with
your whole life ahead of you, large and inexplicable.

It's important: on these mornings you can open the
windows and doors, at least a crack, without freezing or
threatening the planet. Inside goes out, which comes in.
Skins dilate. The thin palisades of the empire of the house
collapse. Here, right by your desk, the French window falls
open from ceiling to floor, like cut ripe wheat.

This gives permission for the morning, the breeze, and
certain shadows to rub against your leg, mindful and
reassuring, with their strange remembered fur.

Cinque Terra, Liguria

Morning moth
in the shower, owl
on the phone line
at nightfall –
two dark-drenched
bookends to the day;

and between them
the *Cinque Terra*,
upthrown tortured cliffs,

vertical
            grape
                        terraces,

great walls stacked
over astonished water

and we –
a boatload of tourists
sunblown and snapping
on the deep blue sea.

Moonlit Walk

for Robert Bly

A walk with you under the powerful, almost-full moon over
the mountains, the valley charged with fine water pinheads
suspended in the air like thought. They spread the light that
swathes the woods and fields and turns the olive trees to
smoke, irresolute at their edges, like people we know who
are somehow neither with us nor absent.

Now, in a clearing, the white horse chews the dark calmly,
its skin moon. It's as if nothing is different here, no change
between this time and others in this place, the same owl-
echo, both late and early, the same steep road snaking up
from the river to the wishful village, strewn with shadows,
patient, just equal to its burdens.

And you – almost fourteen, in your white T-shirt and
unlaced trainers, so excited by sheer simple night; and the
green wink of a jet making its way from near to far, among
the shifting clouds, young stars.

Let's Walk Tonight

Let's walk tonight to Crespiano in the moonlight
along that steep and ancient road
that winds white like a twisted sheet
across the breast of the mountain, down
between the village and the town.

The road will forgive our feet for its beating
since long ago it learned patience –
pilgrims, merchants, soldiers
and animals walked all over it;
it's still here but they are gone.

Squadrons of bats will protect us
from mosquitoes, while owl cries ride
on that pale horse through the trees
and darkness slips over our skin, promiscuous
as oil or spilled wine.

When we arrive we'll have some beer or *gelato,*
the people will toast us
for our failure to understand them,
because where we come from
words are emptied once spoken.

And the dead will keep us company also
relaxed and free from hope
but listening carefully and remembering –
and they'll drink with us too
though their throats are sieves.

Their stories are simple as the trees
that were climbed on by children
who are now old women in the village square
or in the libraries of wood
that lie buried under the world.

They stay until a sudden breeze pours through them
and us, the town's walls open and wave their pages fretfully
like washing in a storm and like the millions
of leaves in the night mountains
all along the road to Crespiano.

How Poetry Can Be Useful – 1

for Phil Connolly

In a well-worn book
of poems by Charles Simic,
loaned to me by a fellow poet
who no doubt thought
I needed some help,
I found an Egyptian
fifty-pound banknote.

The wrinkled old thing
had clearly been battered
by life as an object
of desire. But now,
squeezed in verse
it had become perfectly flat,
like an autumn leaf
ironed by a child
for a school project.

In fact it looked
remarkably calm
for currency.
It was as if poetry
had shown it another world;
taught it, perhaps,
to relax and count
quietly to fifty,
without numbers.

How Poetry Can Be Useful – II

From the lit door
of the yellow house
into Tuscan dusk

a spider in pity
I scoop up and scurry

with a handy book
by Seamus Heaney.

Wave

A wave came through the house;
ravenous, sweeping
all we owned or wished
after that touch in the hallway
and the faces of those we knew
before and then,
away.

After it the place was still,
still was.
Through the open door
onto the dry red carpet
your cat Bella stepped in from the rain.
No thing had been disturbed,
nothing was the same.

This garden today

26th July 2012

has tongues
of Polish and blackbird,
cats and children,
and in the wind

the hedge-loud tenement
of restless birds
who dart like names
lost then re-found

in the faces of flowers
or the imperfect
silence of books.
Love, years

have gone past crazily –
so much so that I have to go
outside, where I'd stand
on my head in the rain

to wed you again,
reminded of the bulk
and bodiness
of our dreams,

and what we hold
in the word-wet world,
the sometimes quiet shouting
of flowers, birds, tongues.

A Drive North in March

Not yet a glint of green, so these hills
are precisely the many dull and beautiful colours
of the small rabbit asleep forever on the long mothering
shoulder of the highway curved under the great sky
and clouds with the texture of sheep and the immensity
of dreams that would run away with you,
if you could run. No,

though Easter is close there's no hint yet of spring,
as if the shameless naked trees had lost the habit, here
where the way passes through the rounded hills
with their winter fur, and we hold the hope at least
that the road goes on and that maybe just around the corner
there'll be a sign that says exactly how far,
and where to. But you,

a kind of rebirth is always in your eyes
in their distances and intimacy, from the deepnesses
of your heart, and your strange girlhood in that place
where now the miners have come up black-faced, grinning,
free of addictions, and never need or want to go down again,
and the fields can just be fields once more,
green, keeping their secrets.

The Hearing

for Dianne

Love, our hedge-sparrows have flown with us on holiday:
they flirt with the locals in the olives by Lake Garda,
wittering in passable Italian, with Yorkshire accents.
On this bright balcony you sleep, I write.
In both worlds the Alps hover between water and sky,
everywhere hegemonies of blue;
and I dreamed an owl last night.
Invented from the windless lake
it flew without sound between the black blades
of the cypresses towards me,
then veered and vanished.
I was not its business.

There's a silence that helps things be heard,
like the one in the mountains yesterday
which shocked with its solitude, since we were far from
    alone. You said
it was as if you'd come home in these blue, high places,
spellbound yet oddly at ease, as you'd been that first time
in Switzerland, when your childhood pit village had given
    you
no words for where you found yourself –
silences and heights, silences and seen distances
into which the heart can fly.
And the belled cattle, like huge poets, with no choice
but to make some kind of music as they move through the
    world,
their echoing metals not breaking the silence, but making it.

Water

i.m. Edward Carr

At a glance, the car
had stopped by the roadside
and the woman was heaving
clothes into the vista
of winter-huge moors.
I drove past

arrived with reluctance.
On the pillow your mouth
a wide-open door, tooth-cave
of the body sucking in the last
of the earth's gifts.
You could not speak – you,

whose next-door laughter
at *Saturday Wrestling*
punched through two feet of millstone
grit, whose prodigal anger bulldogged
privilege, politicians, the painters
of yellow lines on the old roads of England

and terrorised your children.
What was this rage,
sown in a generation
nurtured by poverty, belief betrayed,
exploding again and again,
its secrets never spoken?

Now, in this room full of world
which pushes the world away,
there are no more secrets,
or none that matter. Matter stills,
gets out of shape, collapses
into nothing.

Finally, this is a simple place.
Empty clothes
lay by the road
in the moor wind.
Minutes before the end
you craved water, enjoyed it.

Winter Text

for Hugh

The text flew through cold air, invisible like prayer.
Dutiful Dad, I delivered what was needed –
plastic sheets, scissors, candles, tape –
to the churchyard in the streets' half-light.

There, the pointing gravestones laid flat
for practicality were dulled shapes under snow,
just a few left standing to remind the sky
to be Heaven.

That night's project: three tall snowmen
and an ice house needing a roof, three young faces
on gangly bodies, fast-grown, excited
under the crossed clock tower.

And you – old trees overhead like the arms
of angels reaching up to the dark,
on your childhood's last night,
in the shallow English snow among the graves.

Today

for Owen

Today I'm staking the sunflowers
so they can drink light
and climb as far as they can
in the winds that don't care.

Once, before time,
blown clear of the dead,
they were near to nothing,
bundled in dark arks

just here on the desk
made of a pew hewn
from a pine in a forest
no one can enter;

and long winter months
while I wrote
they seemed mute signs,
like these, but unwritten.

Then they became other, bright,
struck up their own conversations
with the sky, stretched
into its huge strange windows,

hungry for world. And I know
each day this whole business
is messy and comes at you
in riddles. What can one do

and what use are words
when children still cry
out in the distance
next to our skin?

Today I'm staking sunflowers
so they can drink light
and climb as far as they can
in the winds that don't care.

The Gathering

Crisp skin-case
of a windfall orange
from the orchard in Cordoba,
black in the palm as though by fire,
round as a planet.

Next, bottom third
of a clay bottle
picked up in the morning
by the lowered Thames
on a walk with Bridget.

Broken plate of limestone
raised from the Loire,
strong and flat as bone
from an elephant's skull,
the two children watching.

Then plucked flint,
brown-gold, eye-smooth,
shape and size of a crow's head,
the Norfolk shore,
just you and I.

Finally, a disc
of iron thick as a biscuit,
two inches across,
raiment of rust,
a coin with no value
but its own dull
weight, its silence.

This gathered silence:
these hands, these words.

Tree in Snow

Snow, as if the past
remained possibility;

and this bare tree,
solitary, wondrous,
each black branch
etched with white, all
mapped against grey dawn
air, like a planted river;
the outstretched arc
of tributary limbs
feeding sky down.

So come,
lean with me
into the broad estuary
trunk, close your eyes,
recall the warm house
we could always return to,
feet and hands
aching with cold.

And our luck, to be hungry
only for love.

All

Just before dawn
you are in a bright field, a ploughed
and stubbled, slowly sloping field
in late afternoon, in autumn, in England.

You are lying in that field
and two owls are cradling you.
You have lain down, at the edge
of a town, and they have come.

You were worried, as if wounded,
that you would never get up again
in time; that something had been buried
and would stay hidden forever;

that the leaves would fall from those oak trees
and would be the last leaves (they are falling now);
or that you would slip back, happy and lost,
into your childhood.

And they comfort you, these two companions,
their tawny, otherly wings, as you sleep there
on the dark ploughed earth
at the edge of that town,

caressing your face
like a mother's touch,
and telling you,

these low owls,
these slow owls,
that all is well.

And that is all:
and that is all.

On Reading – II

Still
we sit reading.

Cloud script
crosses the pages
of the old mountains.